100 YEARS

THE ROYAL CANADIAN REGIMENT 1883-1983

Ken Bell   C.P. Stacey

COLLIER MACMILLAN CANADA, INC.

Canadian Cataloguing in Publication Data.

Stacey, C. P. (Charles Perry), 1906-
    100 years : the Royal Canadian Regiment 1883-1983

Bibliography: p.

ISBN 0-02-997670-7

1. Canada. Canadian Army. Royal Canadian Regiment –
Anniversaries, etc.   2. Canada. Canadian Army. Royal
Canadian Regiment – History.   I. Bell, Ken, 1914-
II. Title.

UA602.R58S72   356'.1'0971   C82-095253-2

CONTENTS

The concept, research, and development of this record of The Regiment's 100 years of regular and active force service has been conducted with a great deal of dedication and effort on the part of many wonderful and inspired persons. Its humble beginnings as a historical record of the sacrifices of the men who served, supported by their families and friends, can be traced to a sociable conversation in 1980 in which members of The Regimental family were seeking a unique and suitable method by which we could preserve the ways we all feel about the art of soldiering.

The task was formidable. No one can easily express personal and very private feelings about barking drill sergeants major, seemingly unsympathetic superiors, almost intolerable weather conditions, and, in conflict, the ever present thought that someone, somewhere, resented your presence and was doing his damndest to kill you. This book, with epic photographs selected by Lt.-Col. Ken Bell and a soldier's prose composed by Colonel C. P. Stacey, will go a long way toward encapsulating the subjective feelings of the soldier's trials and joys. In a soldier's vernacular the book provides a good gut feeling for what the Queen of Battle is all about.

My thanks go to Ken Bell and Charles Stacey. They have done a superb job.

Special thanks must also be paid to the research team who so painstakingly examined literally hundreds of thousands of photographs; Major Ralph Priestman, Lieutenant Jeff Smith, and Master Corporal Boris Fedoruk. They made the work of Ken Bell so much easier. Miss Barbara Wilson of Public Archives Canada and Miss Patricia Kennedy of Massey College, Toronto, provided valuable assistance to Col. Stacey. We are in debt to The Canadian Forces Photographic Unit, Ottawa, for assistance in the procurement of photos from archives long unused. Mention must also be made of those wonderful archivists and museum curators all across our great country of Canada whose help was invaluable. Finally, I would like to recognize the magnificent response of The Regimental family members who dug back into their albums and family treasuries to resurrect and send along cherished personal photographs.

To all of you, my sincere thanks.
Pro Patria.

Tom Lawson

Tom Lawson
Colonel
Colonel of the Regiment

6

BATTLE HONOURS

Saskatchewan	Mount Sorrel	Passchendaele	Motta Montecorvino	Lamone Crossing
Northwest Canada, 1885	Somme 1916	Amiens	San Leonardo	Rimini Line
Paardeberg	Ancre Heights	Hindenburg Line	Ortona	Italy, 1943–1945
South Africa, 1889–1900	Vimy, 1917	Pursuit to Mons	Hitler Line	North-West Europe, 1945
Ypres 1915, 1917	Hill 70	Landing in Sicily	Gothic Line	Korea, 1951–1953

The Royal Canadian Regiment, Canada's oldest regular infantry unit, has soldiered through 100 years of peace and war in loyal and dedicated service to the nation, the Commonwealth and the free world.

I am proud to say that my association with The Regiment goes back to 8 December 1953 when I had the honour of being appointed Colonel in Chief. By a happy coincidence, I now find that I have completed 30 years as Colonel in Chief at the same time as The Regiment is celebrating its centenary.

The last 100 years have provided plenty of challenges and this volume is a tribute to the men whose discipline and courage created the spirit and the reputation The Regiment enjoys today. The book traces the thread of The Regimental story as it weaves through the tapestry of Canadian and world history. It shows the moments of success and elation and the moments of hardship and sacrifice but most important, it shows the continuity of service and the strong sense of family cohesion which are such vital factors in the life of a regiment.

I am sure this book will give much pleasure to the Old Comrades but I hope it will also be seen and read by many other Canadians and that it will give them an added sense of pride in their heritage.

The Dawn of Majuba Day,
R. Caton Woodville.

AUTHORS' PREFACE

This book was conceived as an opportunity for the members of The Royal Canadian Regiment, past and present, to share the celebration of The Regiment's centenary in 1983 with the people they serve.

It tells the story of The Regiment in text and pictures. The photographs are the result of research in several continents and various countries, which brought to light many old prints that had never been published. On the other hand, few pictures were found concerning some episodes of the story: The Regiment's part in the North West campaign of 1885, or, curiously enough, its activities between the two world wars. No separate sections, therefore, have been devoted to these affairs. Since, however, search turned up a good many photographs of the work of the Yukon Field Force of 1898–1900, a chapter has been included on that unique episode in Canadian military history. On the most recent period, photographs have been taken especially for this book.

We must express our warm thanks to Major R.V. Priestman, CD, who worked with us on behalf of The Regiment.

K.B.
C.P.S.

The Infantry School Corps at Stanley Barracks, Toronto, 1884.

THE CANADIAN REGULAR SOLDIER

On 22 November 1855, in the later stages of the Crimean War, Maj.-Gen. George Wetherall, the adjutant general at the Horse Guards in London, wrote a letter to Colonel Baron de Rottenburg, his opposite number in the Province of Canada. The newly-appointed adjutant general of the Canadian militia was confronting the task of organizing the little force of volunteers — the forerunner of the modern Canadian militia — that the legislature had just authorized. Wetherall had seen a lot of mixed service in Canada (he had commanded the column that had dispersed the Lower Canadian rebels at St. Charles in 1837). After giving some advice on training manuals, he passed on to other matters: "You have an up-hill task before you, & a peculiar people to deal with, a people [who] tho' not quite republican, are tending on it — obstinate in self importance — & consequently difficult to mould into soldierlike shape. The Home Government propose to raise two Regts. in Canada, or the NA Provinces. I am convinced that whatever they may do in N Brunswick & Nova Scotia, they never will be able to raise 1000 men worth having in Canada."

Wetherall was a bad prophet. The scheme of 1855 was not proceeded with, but in 1858 a regular regiment of the British Army, the 100th Royal Canadian Regiment of Foot, with de Rottenburg as its commander, was rapidly and successfully raised in Canada. It was a predecessor, though not a direct ancestor, of Canada's own Royal Canadian Regiment; and it proved that the idea of Canadians as professional soldiers, and good ones, was not chimerical. But it was some time before the peculiar quasi-republican people of Canada had anything like a regular army of their own, and longer before they and their Parliament really accepted the idea.

Insofar as Canada had a military tradition, it was a militia tradition — and one that rather twisted the facts of history. Good Canadians believed that the militia had saved the day in the War of 1812. Before the year 1812 was quite over, in fact, the Rector of York (now Toronto), the Reverend John Strachan, was telling his congregation that the local boys, "without the assistance of men or arms, except a handful of regular troops," had "twice saved the country" (that is, at Detroit and Queenston Heights). Every historian knows that this precisely reversed the facts; it was the "handful of regular troops" and their able and resolute commander, Sir Isaac Brock, that saved Upper Canada with the assistance of the militia. Nevertheless, the legend started by the Reverend Dr. Strachan marched on and was implicitly believed through the decades. It did great harm to Canadian military policy, for it led Canadians to think that in an emergency the country could be adequately defended by untrained lads called from the plough-tail.

Friendly respect for the British redcoat was also part of the Canadian tradition. In 1870–71 the British regulars were finally withdrawn from Canada, except the defended port of Halifax. The only measure the Canadian government took by way of replacing them was to form two small artillery batteries to look after the fortifications at Quebec and Kingston and to train the militia gunners. These units — in due course to be known as the Royal Canadian Horse Artillery — were the earliest nucleus of confederated Canada's regular army. The volunteer militia, thanks to five years of Fenian alarms and the resultant willingness of Parliament to spend some money on the force, had grown in efficiency, but the efficiency declined when the British regiments departed and the military schools that they had run for the volunteers vanished with them. After a dozen years of agitation by people who understood the situation, the Dominion government in 1883 provided the cash to set up permanent instructional units for the other basic arms: an Infantry School Corps, which became The Royal Canadian Regiment, and a Cavalry School Corps, which was the origin of The Royal Canadian Dragoons. Few Canadians, probably, thought of these units as constituting a fighting regular army; yet some of them acted as precisely that in the North West only two years later, and General Middleton was lucky to have them.

Only slowly did the Canadian regular make his way in public esteem. The old militia legend worked against him, and the militia tended to resent him as the recipient of funds that might otherwise have been spent on the citizen force. Moreover, he had to contend with what might be called the ghost of the old British regular garrison. In the eyes of the public, a regular was a *British* regular; the Canadian professional was suspected of being a rather bogus copy. The Militia Act, by which all Canadian soldiers lived until the National Defence Act was passed in 1950, tended to perpetuate the invidious distinction. The Militia Act defined the Permanent Force as "that portion of the Active Militia of Canada permanently embodied for the purpose of providing for the care and protection of forts, magazines, armaments, warlike stores, and other military service, and of securing the establishment of schools for military instruction." When the Act mentions "His Majesty's regular army" it means the British Army; nobody seems to have thought of amending it to reflect the new constitutional situation after the Statute of Westminster was passed in 1931. The word *army*, indeed, was never applied to the military forces of Canada until the Second World War: General H. D. G. Crerar effected the change after he became Chief of the General Staff in 1940. Until then the regulars, like all Canadian military people, were termed *militia*: an ancient and honourable word eminently suitable for a citizen force, but carrying a suggestion of amateurism inappropriate for professionals.

An indication of the low state of the Canadian regular in the eyes of government and Parliament can be seen in the matter of pensions. Though there had been a considerable Permanent Force since 1883, and the militia had had some permanent staff even before Confederation, it was only in 1901 that the first Militia Pension Act, offering a degree of security to members of the force after retirement, was passed. This, surely, was an absolute prerequisite to the development of a genuine professional organization.

The First World War did little to change Canadian military policy or the image of the Permanent Force. The famous Canadian Corps was, of course, a citizen army, which acquired its military expertise on the battlefield; and Canadians at large were merely strengthened in their old belief in the military competence of untrained multitudes. They did not note that Canada could not place a division in the field until seven months after war broke out, and that it took two years for the force to acquire its full strength of four divisions. After the war the Permanent Force remained tiny: two new infantry regiments, Princess Patricia's Canadian Light Infantry, and the Royal 22e Régiment, appeared upon its list, but restricted establishments made it incapable of real military action. The Non-Permanent Active Militia remained the country's first and last line of defence. Canada's security depended on the generosity of her friends and neighbours.

The Second World War was the turning point in the fortunes of the regular army. That the Permanent Force units, recruited to full strength, played important parts on the battlefield was the least of it. Permanent Force officers provided the field army's most senior commanders (though it should not be forgotten that at the end of the war, when many months of fighting experience had blurred the distinction between regular and citizen soldiers, three of Canada's five fighting divisions were commanded by officers from the pre-war non-permanent force). Whereas in the First War the Canadian Corps profited to the end by the services of well-trained staff officers lent by the British Army, in the Second the important staff appointments were filled (particularly in the early days) by officers of the Canadian Permanent Force — who nevertheless had got their training in British staff colleges. The contribution of the Permanent Force's officer corps was out of all proportion to its small size.

When the war was over, Canada did not entirely revert to its former defenceless condition. The army was told it could plan for a regular force of up to 25 000 members (a contrast with the 4000 of 1939). This enabled it to create for the first time a regular mobile striking force of brigade group strength. The responsibilities accepted under the North Atlantic Treaty of 1949 and the outbreak of the Korean War in 1950 led to further expansion. Later came a variety of peace-keeping duties in different parts of the world. Jobs like these could only be done by regular troops; and by 1954 the regular army, with a strength of about 50 000, was for the first time larger than what was now called the Canadian Army (Militia). Canadian regular soldiers were no longer the despised and rejected creatures they had once been. They were recognized as a vital element in the country's public service, well thought of at home and respected in the countries around the globe in which they served.

I
THE BEGINNINGS,
1883-1914

In 1883, when the Canadian government made up its mind to establish a permanent Infantry School Corps, what material was available to work with? As quarters for the three companies that were to make up the Corps, there were the old British barracks at Fredericton, New Brunswick; St. Jean, Quebec; and Toronto, Ontario. As a source of officers there was the militia, including the permanent staff. Selection was strongly influenced by political patronage, but, on the whole, the result was better than the government deserved. Notably, the officer appointed to command the Toronto school, Lt.-Col. W.D. (later General Sir William) Otter, who had been commanding officer of the Queen's Own Rifles, an excellent militia regiment, turned out to be a most fortunate choice. More than any other individual, he was to be the father of professionalism in the Canadian force.

The companies set about recruiting men of military experience, including former British regulars, and almost at once began to take in militia officers and men for instruction. In 1885, before the routine was well established, the permanent corps was called into action to help quell Louis Riel's rebellion in Saskatchewan. Though General Middleton telegraphed from the West asking for all the "regular" units, of the Infantry Corps he got only Otter's C Company from Toronto. Half this company was allotted to Middleton's own column directed on Batoche, the other half to a force under Otter marching on Battleford. The regular infantry-

men were hotly engaged in Middleton's fights at Fish Creek and Batoche (where the rebellion was finally crushed) and in Otter's clash with Poundmaker's Indians at Cut Knife Hill. They suffered nine casualties, of which two were fatal: the names of Bugler H. Foulkes and Private A.J. Watson stand first on a very long regimental roll of honour. In commemoration of this campaign, The Regiment's colours carry the honours "Saskatchewan" and "North West Canada, 1885."

In 1887 the Infantry School Corps acquired a fourth company, stationed in London, Ontario. In 1892 the Corps achieved a new and important status, becoming the Canadian Regiment of Infantry; and in 1893, when Queen Victoria honoured the Canadian permanent corps with the Royal prefix, it became The Royal Regiment of Canadian Infantry. The designation was changed to The Royal Canadian Regiment of Infantry in 1899; and in 1901 The Regiment acquired the name it has borne ever since: The Royal Canadian Regiment. The Regiment had no actual commanding officer until 1896, when Lt.-Col. George J. Maunsell, who had commanded the Fredericton company from the beginning, was appointed. Two years later he was succeeded by Lt.-Col. Otter.

Meanwhile the work of conducting schools of instruction for the militia went steadily on. A fifth regimental station and company, at Quebec City, was authorized in 1899; and in the same year a famous British soldier who had distinguished himself in Can-

At the Citadel in Quebec City, 1905.

ada, Field Marshal Lord Wolseley, accepted the appointment of Honorary Colonel. Occasionally The Regiment was permitted to bring its widely dispersed companies together for a period of battalion training. In 1898 The Royal Regiment of Canadian Infantry contributed the largest component of the Yukon Field Force, a unique enterprise which is described in the next chapter. In the autumn of 1899 the South African War broke out. This conflict involved The Regiment in its first campaign abroad. This also is given a chapter to itself.

The withdrawal of the British Army from Canada, begun in 1870–71, was completed in 1905–6 when the historic defended port and naval base of Halifax and the newer one of Esquimalt, British Columbia, were handed over to Canadian keeping. The Canadian forces now had full responsibility for the security of Canadian territory. This brought new tasks for The Royal Canadian Regiment, which provided the infantry garrison of Halifax. The Regiment was considerably enlarged, some of the new recruits being enlisted from the British Army; it was now to have ten companies, six of which would be in Halifax, the other four being stationed at Quebec City, St. Jean, Toronto, and London, with the primary duty of assisting in training the militia of those areas. By 1908 The Royal Canadian Regiment actually had a strength of slightly over 1000. Thereafter, inevitably, the establishment was reduced.

The year 1908 witnessed a considerable Canadian military occasion: the observances accompanying the Quebec Tercentenary. In the grand review on 24 July, more than 12 000 men of the Canadian regular and citizen forces, in the bright uniforms of those days, marched past the Prince of Wales (afterwards King George V); Brig.-Gen. Otter, now Chief of the General Staff and in command of the parade, reflected that this force was larger than the armies of Wolfe and Montcalm together. By Otter's order, the last unit to swing past was The Royal Canadian Regiment. The Prince inquired why it was not in its proper place at the head of the infantry. Otter's biographer records his modest reply: "I wanted the tail to be equal to the head." The Regimental history gives the Prince's comment: "I see, General, you kept the best wine for me until the end."

Ceremonial magnificence is one part of a regular soldier's life. Much more sordid is another part: "aid to the civil power." In international affairs, when diplomacy fails, war ensues and the soldier takes over. In the life of a nation, when disorder becomes too much for the civil police, the soldier is called in to do a job he hates. In 1909 part of The Regiment, with other units of the Permanent Force, was ordered to Glace Bay, Nova Scotia, where a bitter miners' strike was in progress. This duty stretched out for eight long months; and in 1910 The Regiment was called upon to keep order in another mine strike in Nova Scotia, this time at Springhill.

In Europe tension was growing. War was coming, though few people in Canada realized it, or had any idea of what it would mean for the Dominion. It was true that there was an increase in military activity and in militia expenditure under the auspices of Sam Hughes, Minister of Militia and Defence in Sir Robert Borden's Conservative government that came to power in 1911; but one of Hughes's many eccentricities was a strong dislike of the Permanent Force, and for it little was done. The establishment of The Regiment was actually reduced in 1913, and it is interesting that even the smaller strength could only be attained by recruiting some men in England. The life of a professional soldier apparently still had few attractions for Canadians.

The Regiment went on doing its job. One of its tasks in 1913 was to report on the Ross rifle, an improved version of which had just been issued. The report was unfavourable, but it had no effect. Although the Ross was a legacy from the previous Liberal government, Hughes was devoted to it and would hear no criticism of it. The Regiment's poor opinion of it was to be confirmed by experience on the battlefields of France.

Lt.-Col. William Otter of The Royal Canadian Regiment.

Some of the first recruits to The Infantry School Corps, Fredericton, 1884.

Infantry School Corps band, Fredericton, 1885.

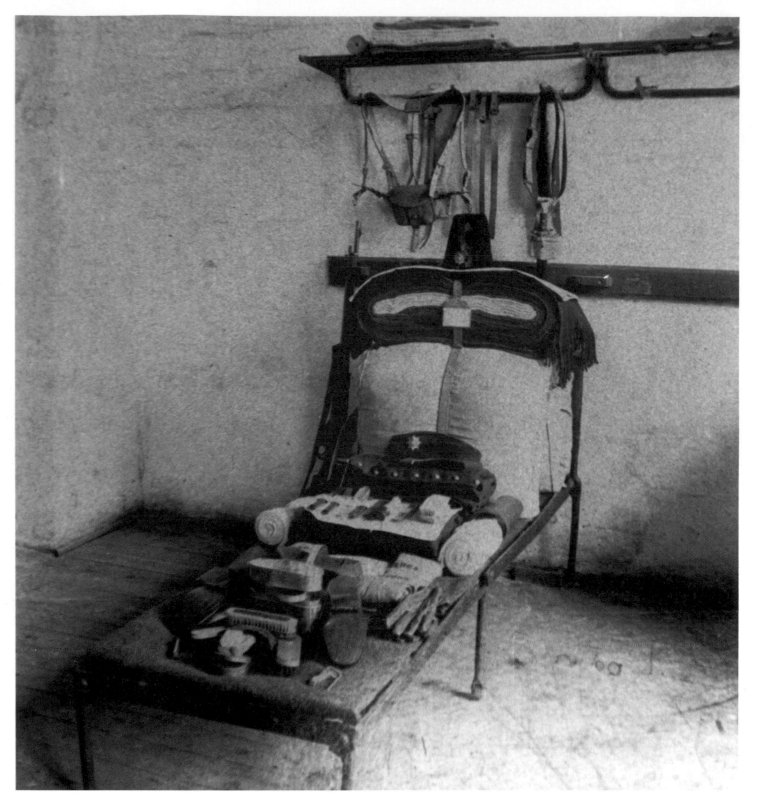

RCR kit layout in barracks, ca. 1880s.

Soldiers relaxing during a picket duty, 1880s.

Physical training, 1880s.

RCR soldiers at the Citadel in Quebec City, ca. 1900.

RCR officers at play, St. Jean, 1905.

Members of C Company training while en route to the North West Rebellion.

Camp life, Petawawa, early 1900s.

Indian leaders surrender at Battleford.

Louis Riel, captured.

The 3rd (Special Service) Battalion of The Royal Canadian Regiment on guard duty at Wellington Barracks, Halifax, 1900.

The 3rd Battalion on parade, Halifax, 1902.

Paardeberg dinner, early 1900s. The victory at Paardeberg is celebrated to this day.

*Captain W.H. Kaye
and his bride.*

Officers' mess, Halifax, 1909.

II
THE TRAIL OF '98
THE YUKON FIELD FORCE

The famous Klondike gold rush involved Canada's permanent military force, and The Royal Regiment of Canadian Infantry in particular, in an unusual adventure.

With thousands of gold seekers from all parts of the world pouring into the distant Yukon Territory, maintaining order and enforcing the law there became heavy tasks. These fell upon the North West Mounted Police, and the manner in which that force discharged them has become legendary. Early in 1898, however, when it was evident that the stream of prospectors was becoming a torrent, the Canadian government decided that the police on the spot required support, and the decision was taken to send 200 soldiers of the regular force into the territory. One of the reasons given the House of Commons for sending troops instead of additional police was characteristic: it was cheaper, for the North West Mounted Police were better paid than the soldiery!

More than half of the Yukon Field Force — three officers and 130 other ranks — came from The Royal Regiment of Canadian Infantry; the rest were provided by The Royal Canadian Artillery and The Royal Canadian Dragoons. All had volunteered for the job. The commander selected was Lt.-Col. T.D.B. Evans of the Dragoons, a former officer of The Royal Regiment of Canadian Infantry. The force was mobilized in Ottawa and left there on 6 May 1898, after being addressed by the Governor General, Lord Aberdeen. It is interesting that five women accompanied it. Four of them were members of the Victorian Order of Nurses, lately organized by the active and public-spirited Lady Aberdeen; the fifth was Faith Fenton, a reporter for the Toronto *Globe,* whose dispatches are one of the sources for the history of the Force.

There were two main routes into the Yukon from outside. One, followed by most of the miners, was through the American ports of Dyea and Skagway and up the White or Chilkoot passes. The other began with a sail up the Stikine River and continued with a long and difficult overland trek to the waters connecting with the upper Yukon River. It was by the Stikine route that the government chose to send the Yukon Field Force. The reasons seem fairly clear. First, the Stikine route was sometimes referred to as the all-Canadian route — though it involved passing through United States territory at the mouth of the river. The Treaty of Washington (1871) guaranteed Canada the free use of the Stikine for commercial purposes. Secondly, at the time the movement was ordered a bill for constructing a railway on this route was before the House of Commons (it was later killed by the Opposition majority in the Senate). The government's decision condemned the Yukon Field Force to one of the toughest marches ever made by Canadian troops.

The steamer *Islander* brought the Force from Van-

". . . one of the toughest marches ever made by Canadian troops."

couver to Wrangell, the American community at the mouth of the Stikine, arriving on 16 May. There it transferred to river steamers, the *Stikine Chief* and *Strathcona,* which carried it in four days to the head of normal navigation at the hamlet of Glenora. Here it unloaded its stores and prepared for the arduous wilderness march ahead. Miss Fenton described the Queen's birthday celebration at Glenora on 24 May: the dress parade, the *feu de joie,* the resounding cheers for the Queen, for the Klondike miners looking on, and (from the miners) for the Yukon Field Force. Pack animals were collected and men given instruction in carrying heavy burdens. The Force's headquarters was to be at distant Fort Selkirk, on the Yukon River near its junction with the Pelly. At the beginning of June an advance party was sent off to construct barracks there. On 9 June the *Stikine Chief* carried the main body of the Force up the Stikine to Telegraph Creek, where the overland trail, such as it was, began. After final preparations the Force began the march overland to Lake Teslin, 150 miles away. It moved in small parties, mules carrying 200-pound loads, the men, 50 pounds.

Lt.-Col. Evans's official report was lost through the ice of the Lewes River in November, and whatever duplicate was sent to Ottawa cannot now be found. But there is a substitute. Lady Aberdeen recorded in her diary receiving a letter from Lt.-Col. Evans, "a good friend of ours and a fine man," describing the overland march, "a weary tramp on foot for 150 miles or rather 200 miles if the actual distance is counted across a terrible country — boulders & huge fallen trees were the least part of the difficulties for the worst part was the horrible swamps through which they had to wade up to their waists. And nothing to eat but hard biscuits, rancid strong bacon & black tea & this in the midst of great heat & under perpetual attack from the biggest bloodthirstiest hordes of mosquitoes. Even Col. Evans who said at the outset that these expeditions always sounded worse than they were ad-

mits that it was very bad . . . He says the Nurses did splendidly & that they were a great comfort for several of the men got ill — some with rheumatic fever. The only solace of which both Col. Evans and Miss Powell [one of the nurses] speak is the glorious scenery & the profusion of flowers of which they have made collections en route. They say that the view from some of the summits they passed over was superb . . . The Nurses say that their clothes & their boots which were intended to last them for three years are completely worn out . . ."

As successive parties reached the head of Lake Teslin and dumped their loads with relief, a new temporary community named Camp Victoria came into existence there. From here the journey would be by water, but Lake Teslin had nothing like the numerous steamers plying the Stikine. There was one steamer just completed, the *Anglian,* the first to sail those waters. On 21 July, Miss Fenton recorded, Lt.-Col. Evans and 80 men embarked in it for the trip to Fort Selkirk. It was hoped that it would be able to return for the balance of the Force, but in case it failed to do so the troops were set to work constructing craft of their own — five boats and four large scows. It was as well they did, for the *Anglian* did not reappear; it had struck a rock and had to be repaired. On 29 August the improvised flotilla set off down Lake Teslin. The route led down the Teslin River (then sometimes called the Hootalinqua) and on down the Lewes, which on today's maps appears as an upper reach of the Yukon. The formidable Five Fingers Rapids were negotiated without disaster, and on 11 September the main body of the Force landed at Fort Selkirk.

Here the advance parties had made good progress in constructing a new military post, a dozen log buildings around a parade square. Most of the Force remained at this isolated place for the winter. But Superintendent Sam Steele, commanding the Mounted Police in the Yukon, had asked for help at Dawson, the centre of the gold diggings. Here an instant city of some 20 000 people, not all of them particularly desirable citizens, had sprung into existence. Early in October a detachment of 50 men of the Yukon Field Force was sent down the Yukon by steamer to Dawson. No doubt their presence there was partly responsible for the remarkably good order that reigned in Dawson throughout this time of crisis and excitement. The Yukon Field Force, in fact, was never called upon for more than routine security duties.

Late in the summer of 1899, half the Force was withdrawn, and Lt.-Col. Evans was succeeded in the command by Major T.D.R. Hemming of The Royal Canadian Regiment of Infantry. The headquarters of the Force was moved from Selkirk to Dawson. In 1900, when the critical period of the gold rush was over, the rest of the Force (which had lately been redesignated the Yukon Garrison) left for the outside. The journey home was luxurious compared with the march into the territory in 1898: it was made by riverboat to Whitehorse, and thence by train over the lately-completed White Pass and Yukon Railway to Skagway.

The Yukon Field Force deserves to be remembered chiefly for that march of 1898. The General Officer Commanding the Militia, Maj.-Gen. Edward Hutton, paid tribute to the "perseverance, persistence of purpose, endurance and discipline under trying circumstances" displayed during this movement across "an hitherto but little known and very difficult country." It recalled, he said, Lord Wolseley's famous Red River expedition of 1870.

The Yukon Field Force on parade, probably in Dawson City.

Members of the Yukon Field Force aboard the Stikine Chief.

The Yukon Field Force relaxing in camp.

Lt.-Col. T.D.B. Evans in camp.

Members of the Yukon Field Force building craft for the trip down Lake Teslin.

An advance party of the Force building the headquarters at Fort Selkirk during the summer of 1898.

Lt.-Col. Evans, commander of the Yukon Field Force.

"On 29 August the improvised flotilla set off down Lake Teslin."

New guard presenting arms, Dawson City, 1899.

III
THE SOUTH AFRICAN WAR

War, long threatened, broke out between Britain and the two Boer republics in South Africa in October 1899. British colonies around the globe offered contingents to the mother country. The Canadian people and the Canadian government were divided — primarily on the basis of English versus French — as to what the country should do. The final decision was to offer a contingent of volunteers, defined as "a regiment of infantry, 1000 strong, under command of Lt.-Col. Otter." The British government had suggested small units of 125 men to be scattered through the British Army; it was the Governor General, Lord Minto, who insisted that the force should be "a Canadian contingent to act as such" under a senior Canadian officer. It was a precedent of some importance.

It may perhaps have been Otter himself who suggested that the force he was to command should be designated as a unit of the Dominion's regular infantry regiment; and it was mobilized as the 2nd (Special Service) Battalion of The Royal Canadian Regiment of Infantry, which was already being spoken of as simply The Royal Canadian Regiment. Eight companies were quickly raised by volunteering from 82 different units of the militia across Canada from Charlottetown to Victoria. It is a point of importance that about 150 of the men came from the Permanent Force, which contributed 13 of the 41 officers, eight of them from The Royal Canadian Regiment.

To a modern eye the thing that is remarkable about this affair is that the battalion sailed for South Africa just sixteen days after the order to recruit the companies was issued, and that only about four months after that order it joined a regular British brigade and fought successfully in a major battle: this in spite of the fact that Otter reported that "a very large number" of his men when they enlisted were "ignorant of the first principles" of soldiering. The explanation, doubtless, lies partly in the fact, also noted by Otter, that the raw material was good: he speaks of the men's excellent physiques and "high intelligence." But one suspects that a more important element in the situation was the fairly large proportion of experienced regular soldiers in the battalion. In particular, a probably vital point was that the senior non-commissioned officer of every company (*colour sergeants* in the usage of those days) was a regular. Seven of the eight were from The Regiment. These colour sergeants undoubtedly played a major part in licking the raw material into the shape that enabled the unit to go into action at a time when the men might still have been regarded as recruits.

The battalion landed at Cape Town on 30 November 1899. It was at once ordered up-country, but not into the front line. It spent some weeks on the lines

Lt.-Col. Otter (centre) and officers of the 2nd (Special Service) Battalion of The Royal Canadian Regiment.

of communication, improving its training and getting useful experience. One company was engaged with other units in a minor operation against a Boer pocket of resistance at Sunnyside, but suffered no casualties. The arrival of Field Marshal Lord Roberts in South Africa to take command indicated that a large offensive movement was imminent; and in mid-February 1900 The Royal Canadian Regiment moved to Gras Pan to join the 19th Infantry Brigade, then being formed under the command of Maj.-Gen. Horace Smith-Dorrien. The brigade's other units were battalions of the Duke of Cornwall's Light Infantry, the King's Shropshire Light Infantry and the Gordon Highlanders. It was a good brigade with an excellent commander, and it earned a high reputation. Sir Arthur Conan Doyle, then in South Africa with the medical service, wrote later that the 19th was "probably the very finest brigade in the whole army."

Advancing with a powerful force of four divisions, Lord Roberts manoeuvred the Boer general Piet Cronje's army out of the position at Magersfontein where it had bloodily defeated a British attack some weeks before, and pinned it down in the valley of the Modder River at Paardeberg Drift (ford). The Boers dug themselves into both banks of the river with great skill, and though they were very heavily outnumbered and outgunned, evicting them was not easy. In the beginning, the British, forgetting earlier encounters that had proved the futility of frontal attacks in the face of the deadly Boer rifles, made this same mistake again. On 21 February the Duke of Cornwall's Light Infantry made an attack that had apparently been ordered by Lord Kitchener, Roberts's chief of staff, without any information of it reaching the brigade commander. The Canadians joined in. The attack withered under the Boer fire; 18 men of The Regiment were killed that day, and two others, including one officer, later died of wounds.

There were no more unco-ordinated and unsupported daylight attacks. For the next five days the British artillery pounded the Boer positions, and, while their deep trenches gave the Boers good protection, it was doubtless the British bombardment that prepared the way for victory. February 27 would be the nineteenth anniversary of the Boer defeat of the British at Majuba Hill in 1881, and for the nights preceding this, the British trenches had been advanced closer and closer to Cronje's position until the time for the final assault had come. The RCR was holding the front line on the night of the 26–27, and it fell to it to strike the blow. At 2:15 a.m. the silent advance began. The battalion was within 100 yards of the enemy trenches when a sudden storm of fire came down on it. The men threw themselves down and began to dig in. Someone unknown shouted an order to retire, and the men on the left obeyed it; but the two companies on the right, along with some Engineers, held on. At dawn, well entrenched, they opened close-range fire on the Boers. This was the end. White flags began to appear in the Boer position, and shortly afterwards Cronje surrendered with his force of 4000 men. The RCR had lost 13 men killed and 36 wounded. It was the first great British victory and the turning point of the war. It is not surprising that The Regiment still celebrates Paardeberg Day.

Lord Roberts now advanced on Bloemfontein, the capital of the Orange Free State. The Boers tried but failed to check him at Poplar Grove, and the British, including the Royal Canadians, marched into Bloemfontein on 15 March. Late in April the 19th Brigade was incorporated into a force commanded by General Ian Hamilton that operated against Boer forces east of Bloemfontein. In an engagement at Israel's Poort, Lt.-Col. Otter was slightly wounded and Lt.-Col. Lawrence Buchan, the second-in-command, took over. On 30 April there was a tough little fight at Thaba Mountain, which cost The Regiment one man killed and six wounded. The British force now moved north. It had to fight for the crossing of the Zand River on 10 May. Roberts proceeded to invade the South African Republic (also called the Transvaal). The Boers fought fiercely in a covering position at Doorn Kop, and The Regiment had seven wounded here on 29 May. Finally, on 5 June The Regiment entered the republic's capital, Pretoria, as part of Roberts's victorious army.

Many people thought that with both Boer capitals in British hands the war was over. They were wrong. The stubborn Boers merely resorted to guerrilla warfare, and their resistance was not finally beaten down until 1902. The Regiment's part in the war, however, was nearly ended. In August it engaged in operations against isolated Boer columns. But the Canadians had volunteered for "six months, or one year if required." The year was nearly over, the war seemed to be likewise, and when the men were asked to extend their service the majority of them, almost inevitably, declined. Other Canadian units wore the maple leaf in South Africa during the guerrilla phase of the war. The 2nd Battalion of The Regiment embarked for home from Cape Town on 7 November 1900.

The trip to Canada was roundabout and eventful. Reaching England on 29 November, the battalion was given a truly royal welcome. It was feted in London and entertained to the point of exhaustion. The high point, however, was a trip to Windsor Castle, where the Canadians were inspected and thanked by Queen Victoria, aged 81 and already legendary. It was one of her last public appearances; she died less than two months later. The Royal Canadians finally reached Halifax two days before Christmas. There the 2nd (Special Service) Battalion was at once disbanded. Sixty-eight of its officers and men had died on service; illness had killed nearly as many as Boer bullets. It bequeathed to The Regiment memories of gallantry and sacrifice, the campaign honour "South Africa, 1899–1900" and the proud battle honour "Paardeberg."

The Regiment made one other contribution to this war. In March 1900 a Canadian battalion of 1000 men was raised to replace the infantry garrison of Halifax, thus freeing a British battalion for war service. The new unit was designated the 3rd (Special Service) Battalion of The Royal Canadian Regiment, and its efficiency owed much to officers and men drawn from the parent unit. It did duty until September 1902, when a British battalion arrived at Halifax to relieve it.

Officers from one of the later Canadian contingents before leaving for South Africa.

Officers of C Company sailing to South Africa on the troopship Sardinian, *1899.*

Lt.-Col. Buchan, second-in-command of The Regiment in South Africa, 1900.

The RCR crossing the Modder River on the way to Paardeberg Drift.

*Attacking
the enemy.*

Some of the 4000 Boer prisoners captured at Paardeberg.

Overleaf: After Paardeberg.

A rare carefree moment during the South African War.

At Windsor Castle the Royal Canadians are inspected and thanked by Queen Victoria.

On the way home, Liverpool Station.

The 2nd Battalion returning from South Africa, 23 December 1900.

October 1909. The funeral in Montreal of Brigadier Buchan,
former second-in-command of the 2nd (Special Service) Battalion in South Africa.

IV
THE FIRST WORLD WAR

Historians, with the invaluable benefit of hindsight, can chart what seems now the inexorable approach of the European war of 1914; but to the people of distant, peaceful Canada that summer the outbreak came like an unexpected thunderclap. The assassination of an Austrian archduke on 28 June was not recognized as the match lighting the fuse; and it was only when shooting actually began at the end of July that even the government in Ottawa perceived the likelihood of a conflict that was going to be the most important event in Canadian history.

The Dominion's one regular infantry regiment was, needless to say, in a much higher state of readiness for war than the country at large. On 31 July The Royal Canadian Regiment's companies in Halifax moved to the posts in the port's defences prescribed in the existing defence scheme. Shortly afterwards the companies from inland stations began to arrive to complete the pattern. Even before Britain declared war the Canadian government had offered an expeditionary force, and The Regiment naturally expected to form part of it; but the unexpected happened. On 20 August The Royal Canadian Regiment was officially invited (under the Militia Act it could hardly have been ordered) to volunteer to replace a British battalion garrisoning Bermuda. The Regiment could not refuse, and

from September 1914 it did duty in that quiet Atlantic colony. Only in August 1915 was The Regiment relieved by another Canadian unit and allowed to take its proper place in Canada's fighting line overseas.

The Regiment arrived in France that November, under the command of Lt.-Col. A.H. Macdonell. The 3rd Canadian Division was then in the process of formation; soon The Regiment was incorporated in it as a unit of the 7th Canadian Brigade. The 7th was to be a worthy successor of the famous 19th in South Africa; but it was of course all-Canadian. In addition to The Royal Canadian Regiment, the 7th Brigade was composed of Princess Patricia's Canadian Light Infantry, formed originally from veteran soldiers, and the first Canadian unit to reach France; the 42nd Battalion of the Canadian Expeditionary Force, Royal Highlanders of Canada, the "Canadian Black Watch"; and the 49th Battalion C.E.F., the Edmonton Regiment. In January 1916 The Regiment for the first time took over a portion of the front line, in the Kemmel sector. It was the beginning of nearly three years of trench warfare, miserable and deadly.

Those years cannot be described in detail here. In March 1916 the Canadian Corps, including the 3rd Division, moved to the ill-omened Ypres Salient. The Regiment was now commanded by Lt.-Col. C.H. Hill. The fierce German attack at Mount Sorrel in June cost

". . . a conflict that was going to be the most important event in Canadian history."

63

The Regiment many casualties and earned for it its first battle honour of this war. In September the Corps was moved south to take part in the British offensive on the Somme, which had begun on 1 July. It was a sanguinary and unproductive business. For The Regiment the unsuccessful attack on Regina Trench on 8 October, part of what is called officially the Battle of Ancre Heights, was particularly grim; when it was over The Regiment was down to 140 officers and men. That month the Canadian Corps was transferred to the front facing imposing Vimy Ridge, where The Regiment was built up to strength and the Corps began training for the great operation against the ridge.

The attack went in on 9 April 1917, Easter Monday. The four Canadian divisions, attacking all together for the first time, were disposed in numerical order from right to left; thus the 3rd was in the left centre. The RCR reached its first objective with little trouble; thereafter opposition was heavier, but the final objective on the crest of the ridge was taken almost on time. The 4th Division did not succeed in taking the highest point, where the Canadian memorial now stands, until the following day. In the meantime The Regiment suffered from fire from this high ground. It was relieved and withdrawn on 11 April. The next day the 4th Division took "The Pimple," a northern extension of the ridge. Careful preparation had paid its usual dividends, and the Canadians had won a brilliant victory, which shone the more brightly amid the general gloom of the Western Front. Yet it had been very costly: The Regiment had lost 57 officers and men killed or died of wounds, 155 wounded, and 65 missing.

The 3rd Division was not engaged in the Corps' capture of Hill 70 on 15 August, but after it relieved the 1st and 2nd Divisions in the line it suffered from heavy enemy bombardment. In October the Canadian Corps moved back to the Ypres sector. Here since the end of July Sir Douglas Haig, the British Commander-in-Chief, had been conducting an offensive, often called the Third Battle of Ypres. This operation, persisted in long after hopes of decisive success had faded, was originally intended to cut through to the Belgian coast and eliminate German submarine bases there. As it proceeded the weather grew worse and so did the condition of the ground; it became the "battle in the mud" of evil memory. Successive formations were fed into the grinder, and in October, when conditions were at their worst, the British command resorted to the Canadian Corps. The limited objective now was the low eminence called the Passchendaele Ridge. The 3rd and 4th Divisions went in first. In the 7th Brigade The Royal Canadian Regiment was detailed as support and carrying battalion, sending platoons to reinforce the two attacking units as required. Even in this relatively secondary role its losses were heavy. Early in November the 1st and 2nd Divisions took over. The Canadians took the ridge, but paid a terrible price. The account graven in stone in the Peace Tower in Ottawa records, "the Corps returned to the Lens [Hill 70] sector, having gained two square miles at a cost of 16,404 casualties."

In March 1918 the Germans unleashed their last great offensive and gained much ground. The Canadian front was not attacked, and, when the enemy effort was spent and the Allies were ready to begin their counteroffensive, the Canadian Corps was in prime condition to be a spearhead. It moved secretly to the Amiens front and on 8 August the Canadians and Australians struck the enemy a tremendous surprise blow, so successful that General Ludendorff, in a famous phrase, called this "the black day of the German Army." The RCR, on the Corps' extreme right, took all its objectives with losses much smaller than those that had become so painfully familiar. This was the beginning of the famous Hundred Days of Canadian advances and victories ending in the Armistice. The Regiment had heavier casualties in the offensive in the Arras sector later in August. Then September brought the beginning of the struggle known officially as the Battles of the Hindenburg Line.

Particularly notable in the annals of The Regiment

was the Battle of the Canal du Nord, begun on 27 September 1918. On the second day The Regiment attacked the formidable Marcoing Line, part of the Hindenburg system. D Company found its way blocked by heavy uncut wire, but the company commander, Lieutenant M.F. Gregg, went forward alone and found a small gap. Under heavy fire he led his men through and obtained a foothold in the Marcoing position which was then expanded. Other companies, overcoming fierce resistance, penetrated the line at other points. A shell struck battalion headquarters, badly wounding the commanding officer, now Lt.-Col. C.R.E. Willets, and killing the adjutant, Captain F.D. McCrea. Major C.B. Topp of the 42nd Battalion, who was visiting The Regiment at the time, took over temporarily. It was a bloody but glorious day for The Regiment. On this and the three following days it suffered nearly 300 casualties. Lieut. Gregg, who had already won the Military Cross and a bar, was awarded the Victoria Cross.

The new commanding officer was Lt.-Col. G.W. MacLeod, who came to The Regiment from the 49th Battalion. Under his command The Regiment pushed forward in the series of triumphant operations com-memorated on the colours by the honour "Pursuit to Mons." The trenches were behind now; it was open warfare, and there were actually days when The Regiment advanced with the senior officers mounted and the band playing. The Germans still resisted, but the resistance tended to take the form of demolitions covered by fire. The Regiment suffered its last fatal casualties of the war on 10 November, when a platoon trying to make its way over a wrecked bridge came under fire from a concealed machine gun. By the next day The Regiment was in Mons, where the British Army had first met the Germans in 1914. The Armistice that the beaten enemy had accepted came into effect at 11 a.m. Although the 42nd Battalion has argued the question, it appears that the first troops to reach the Hotel de Ville were a platoon of The Royal Canadian Regiment commanded by Lieutenant W.M. King, who signed the *Golden Book* of Mons to mark the occasion.

What that generation called simply the Great War was over. The price of victory had been heavy. The Royal Canadian Regiment had suffered 3113 casualties; 33 officers and 671 other ranks had lost their lives.

Lt.-Col. Carpenter, commander of The Regiment in Bermuda, and his bride, 1915.

Officers of The Royal Canadian Regiment in winter dress, 1914.

". . . trench warfare, miserable and deadly."

First aid in the trenches, 1916.

A soldier in the mud.

A shell burst wounding a soldier, 1916.

Over the top.

Into the wire.

On the Western Front, 1917.

At Vimy Ridge the four Canadian divisions attacked together for the first time.

The rum ration, France, 1917.

A mortarman from The Regiment, *1917.*

A captured gun.

A winter patrol in no man's land, France, 1917.

The Somme—"a sanguinary and unproductive business."

Death in the mud.

German prisoners help carry the wounded to the rear.

A Canadian soldier at the Somme, 1916.

V
THE SECOND WORLD WAR

Like the annals of the poor, those of The Royal Canadian Regiment between the two world wars are short and simple. Here they must be short indeed. The stages of postwar reorganization need not be described; but by the end of 1924 The Regiment was settled into something like a permanent pattern, with headquarters at London, Ontario, and companies in London, Halifax, Toronto, and St. Jean. The authorized strength was only a little over 400 officers and men. The old routine of instructing the militia, in summer camps and by running "Royal Schools," was again well established. And already The Regiment had had spells of the unpopular strike duty. Everything, it seemed, was as before.

Occasional notable facts stand out: the establishment of the alliance with The Gloucestershire Regiment of the British Army (28th and 61st Foot); the appointment of the Duke of Connaught (who had been Honorary Colonel since soon after Lord Wolseley's death in 1913) as Colonel in Chief; and the celebration of The Regiment's fiftieth anniversary in 1933. The Depression after 1929 brought inevitable economies — and episodes such as one in 1933, when 120 men of The Regiment, with four machine gun carriers, duly reported in the press as tanks, were sent to Stratford, Ontario, to keep order during strikes. These were hard times for most people. But worse troubles were on the

way; that year witnessed the rise of Adolf Hitler to power in Germany.

As the menace in Europe grew, even Canada began to take precautions. Prime Minister Mackenzie King, mustering his courage to defy hostile elements within his own party, brought in a very modest rearmament program. Evidence of a new spirit was the fact that in the summer of 1938 a considerable part of the Permanent Force, including all the companies of The Regiment, with some militia units, was concentrated at Camp Borden, Ontario, for collective field training. Indications of advancing modernity were co-operation by aircraft of the Royal Canadian Air Force and the participation of Canada's first tanks — both of them. September 1939 brought the long-feared outbreak.

The Regiment was in worse shape for war than in 1914. A unit of only 400 men, scattered across the country, had to be recruited up to double that strength; and regular units, reputed to cultivate strict discipline, were not attractive to some prospective soldiers. However, in London The Canadian Fusiliers, who were not themselves being mobilized, made a valuable contribution, including a dozen officers in the first six months. The RCR was soon complete and concentrated at Valcartier. This time it was to have its rightful place in the order of battle from the beginning, as the senior battalion in the 1st Canadian Infantry Brigade

Bren gunner, Italy, 1943.

83

and the 1st Canadian Division. The other units of the brigade were from the Non-Permanent Active Militia, the 48th Highlanders of Canada from Toronto and a solid rural regiment from eastern Ontario, The Hastings and Prince Edward Regiment. The divisional commander was Maj.-Gen. A.G.L. McNaughton, the well-loved "Andy." The division crossed the Atlantic in two flights; The Regiment was on the second, landing in Scotland on 30 December 1939 and moving at once to Aldershot, Hampshire.

What followed was three and a half years of training in Britain. It had been assumed that the division would go to France to fight with the British Expeditionary Force; but the early summer of 1940 brought Allied disaster and the hasty withdrawal of the BEF to England. The 1st Brigade actually saw France for a couple of eventful days in June, as part of an attempt to constitute a "Second BEF" to help save Britain's ally from collapse; it was too late, the brigade was pulled out, and the rest of the division never sailed. The RCR was lucky enough to leave nobody behind — even the two men who threatened desertion to join the Foreign Legion to fight the Germans (they found the Legion was not recruiting just then). Back in England, the Canadians prepared actively to resist an invasion; but it never came. During the long months that ensued, the men of The Regiment became well acquainted with Surrey, and Sussex, and other parts of England's green and pleasant land.

Action came, finally, in 1943. The Germans had been cleared out of North Africa, and as the result of Canadian government pressure the 1st Division was given a share in the next phase — the invasion of Sicily. The division was now commanded by Maj.-Gen. G.G. Simonds, who had succeeded Maj.-Gen. H.L.N. Salmon, an officer of The Regiment, who died tragically in an air crash during the planning period. The Royal Canadian Regiment landed on the division's extreme right on 10 July, and won the division's first decorations for gallantry in assaulting an Italian

battery. In general, however, the Italian opposition was light. When the Germans were met five days after the landing, resistance stiffened. At Nissoria on 24 July The Regiment suffered its first severe check, and the commanding officer, Lt.-Col. R.M. Crowe, leading from in front in the old-fashioned way, was killed. Major T.M. Powers took command. There was hard slogging until the second week of August, when the Canadians were withdrawn from the line. At this point Lt.-Col. D.C. Spry arrived to take over the unit. The last Germans left Sicily on 17 August.

On 3 September 1943 the British Eighth Army, with the 1st Canadian Division in the van, made the leap across the Strait of Messina to the toe of the Italian boot — the mainland of Europe. There was virtually no initial opposition, but this was the beginning of a long, tough battle up the length of Italy, a battle that ended only with the European war itself. Enemy demolitions slowed the advance. The Regiment's first serious contact with the enemy was at Motta Montecorvino on 1–2 October. The redoubtable 1st German Parachute Division inflicted 31 casualties on The Regiment before withdrawing. After advancing over 300 miles since crossing the strait, the 1st Division was glad of a month's rest in the Campobasso area before undertaking another task. British formations having broken the German defence line along the Sangro River, the enemy made his next stand on the Moro River. On 8 December The Regiment attacked from a bridgehead established by The Hastings and Prince Edward, but only after two days of desperate fighting did the Germans give up the Moro Line and the fiercely contested village of San Leonardo. The official historian, Colonel Nicholson, wrote, "In the little farm beside the bend in the road atop the Moro plateau the passing years would heal the splintered olive trees and bring repair to bullet-scarred walls, and not much would remain to remind an Abruzzi peasant that a battle had passed through his orchards and vineyards. Perhaps he might never know that by a few Canadians his house would be remembered as 'Sterlin Castle' [after Lieutenant M. Sterlin, whose platoon held the house against the paratroopers], and the narrow road along which he journeyed to the sea, 'Royal Canadian Avenue'."

The German withdrawal brought little respite; it was necessary to drive on and evict the enemy from his defences covering the port of Ortona. The obstacle here was "The Gully," a ravine running across the front; The Regiment suffered very heavily in battling across it on 18 and 19 December. The 2nd Brigade went on to clear Ortona in house to house fighting, while the 1st pushed the enemy back west of the town. It was a bloody Christmas. Major Strome Galloway, who had seen as much of the business as anybody, wrote later, "During the three weeks of fighting preceding New Year's Day it can truthfully be said that the old regiment had almost passed away." Early in January 1944 a peace of exhaustion settled on the Adriatic front.

At this point Lt.-Col. Spry was promoted, being succeeded in command of The Regiment by Lt.-Col. W.W. Mathers, who in turn was succeeded by Lt.-Col. J.W. Ritchie in June. In the spring the scene moved west of the Apennines. The weight of the Eighth Army was secretly shifted across the mountains for a great offensive towards Rome. There was now a Canadian Corps in Italy and the 1st Division was operating under it. The attack went in on 11 May. The Canadian Corps came into action after the enemy's front position was broken. Its task was to smash through a formidable second line across the Liri valley, which the Germans had called the Fuehrer Riegel until Hitler objected to having his title attached to a position likely to be broken; the Allies called it the Hitler Line. The 1st Division made the assault on 23 May. On the left flank the 48th Highlanders had gained a foothold in the line the previous day. They enlarged it now and The Regiment went through and took the town of Pontecorvo without heavy loss. The next major enemy defence system was the Gothic Line, reaching across Italy from Pesaro to south of Spezia. The Eighth Army, in the Adriatic sector, launched the attack on 30 August. The Regiment entered the fight on 2 September, by which time the main Gothic defences had been pierced, but met fierce opposition on the coast, suffering 155 casualties in four days. Pushing on, the 1st Division, after further costly fighting, broke the Rimini Line, the Germans' last prepared position.

Ahead lay the level Lombard Plain, through which the Po River ran. On the map it looked as though the worst was over. But the map was deceptive. After rain the plain became a sea of mud; and it was traversed by a series of rivers running between high artificial floodbanks, lethal obstacles when contested by a determined enemy. For The Regiment a tough fight on the Pisciatello in October was the prelude to a disaster in December. The 1st Brigade, trying to establish a bridgehead across the Lamone River, fell victim to mismanagement on more than one level and a fierce and skilful German counterattack. Both The Regiment and the Hastings had tragic losses. Inevitably there was a flurry of dismissals. Lt.-Col. W.W. Reid, who had distinguished himself in command of the Perth Regiment in the Gothic Line battle, took over The Regiment and commanded it until the end of the war. The Senio River marked the Canadians' furthest advance in Italy. In February 1945 the 1st Canadian Corps began the long move to join First Canadian Army in northwest Europe. By 16 March The Regiment was in the Belgian village of Schilde, not far from Antwerp.

The Regiment's campaign in the new theatre was brief, for the war with Germany was almost over. On 12 April it crossed the Ijssel River and on the seventeenth the 1st Brigade took Apeldoorn, after meeting slight resistance. It was The Royal Canadian Regiment's last fighting in this war. It had suffered only 61 casualties in northwest Europe, a small toll compared with that in Italy. When the Germans surrendered on 5 May 1945 The Royal Canadian Regiment had lost 370 officers and men killed, 1207 wounded.

Many officers of The Regiment had held high commands and staff appointments during the war. Only a very few can be mentioned. Lt.-Gen. Charles Foulkes had commanded the 1st Corps and became Chief of the General Staff at the end of hostilities. Four major generals commanded divisions: George Kitching (a former officer of the Glosters who joined The Regiment in 1939); D.C. Spry; H.L.N. Salmon; and General Foulkes before he attained higher rank. Lieut. M.F. Gregg, who had won the VC with The Regiment in the First War, served again with it in the Second, rose to the rank of brigadier and held important appointments. Finally, one must remember Brigadier J.K. Lawson, who died fighting, pistol in hand, while commanding the Canadian brigade that took part in the hopeless defence of Hong Kong: a heroic figure who may stand as a type of his Regiment's service through six years of war.

The RCR marching to the Peel Street Barracks, Montreal, 29 October 1919.

Guard of Honour for Arlington Cemetery, composed of The Royal Canadian Regiment and The Royal 22e Régiment, Princes' Gate, Toronto, 1927.

At Stanley Barracks, Toronto, 1919.

Major Milton F. Gregg, who won the Victoria Cross for leading his men through the Marcoing Line in 1918, carries the colour in 1927.

The Duke of Connaught, Colonel in Chief of The Royal Canadian Regiment, reviews Old Comrades, 1933.

King Edward VIII, accompanied by Milton Gregg, at the unveiling of the Canadian War Memorial, Vimy, France, 1936.

Major Strome Galloway and troops sailing to England.

King George VI inspects The Royal Canadian Regiment at Aldershot, England.

A break during training in England, 1942.

Lt.-Col. D.C. Spry, commanding officer in Sicily.

Pioneer Platoon (RCR), Sicily.

Lt.-Gen. McNaughton addressing the troops after their arrival in Sicily.

Sicily.

A mortar platoon at work, Sicily.

Sicily.

Reviewing positions,
Sicily.

Mail call, Sicily.

Soldiers of The Regiment mending their boots, Sicily.

Lineup for water, Italy, 1944.

Troops moving into position, Italy.

Transporting supplies, Italy.

Transporting mortar ammunition, Italy.

"... the beginning of a long, tough battle up the length of Italy, a battle that ended only with the European war itself."

Overleaf: Artillery support, Italy.

The RCR entering Campobasso, 1943.

A Night Raid,
H.J. Mowat.
(First World War)

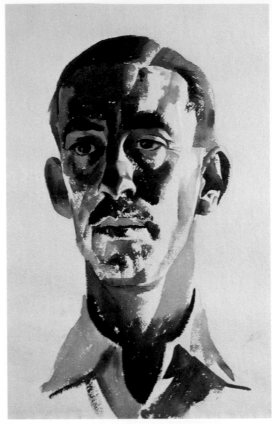

Brigadier D.C. Spry, C.F. *Comfort.*

Private J.W. Gardner MM, C.F. *Comfort.*

Captain R.M. Dillon, MC, C.F. *Comfort.*

Rimini as Approached
on 'Sun' Route, *T.R.
MacDonald.*

German Knocked-Out
Tank, *T. R. MacDonald.*

The Hitler Line, C.F. *Comfort.*

A section of The Regiment
cut down by machine gun
fire at the Moro River,
December 1943.

". . . only after two days
of desperate fighting did
the Germans give up
the Moro Line . . ."

Germans defending Ortona, 1943.

Throwing a grenade, San Leonardo, December 1943.

*Ortona, Italy. "During the three weeks of fighting preceding New Year's Day
it can truthfully be said that the old regiment had almost passed away."*

Firing at a tank.

The liberation of an Italian village.

An old peasant woman spinning wool; a Canadian soldier on patrol.

Italian refugees.

Italy.

General Crerar, Maj.-Gen. Spry, and Field Marshal Montgomery, Holland.

Dutch refugees.

Canadian sniper.

Canadian soldiers advancing to the line, Holland.

Dead German soldiers.

Rescue team, Holland.

Street fighting in Holland, 1945.

A captured German soldier, Holland.

German POW.

Hungry civilians.

A collaborator goes to his death.

Within six hours, 3190 Germans were disarmed near Ijmuiden, Holland.

Captain C.J.A. Aylen-Parker of The Royal Canadian Regiment at the disarming of German prisoners near Ijmuiden, Holland.

131

VI
KOREA

The Second World War, unlike the First, had an effect on Canadian military policy. The country never wholly returned to the defenceless posture of the inter-war years. (If evidence is needed, one might cite the statistics of defence expenditure: before the war, even after rearmament had begun, the annual total ran about $33 million; after the war, it never fell below $195 million.) It is true that Prime Minister Mackenzie King regarded these large figures with dislike: he recorded in his diary on 3 January 1947 that he had told the Cabinet, "What we needed now was to get back to the old Liberal principles of economy, reduction of taxation, antimilitarism, etc." But King soon retired, and world events prevented the revival of his old principles. In 1949 Canada signed the North Atlantic Treaty, and as a result of it Canadian forces soon returned to Europe; 1950 brought the Korean War.

What did all this mean for The Royal Canadian Regiment? It meant, in the earliest postwar years, that it was one, strong, increasingly battleworthy battalion (stationed, at first, at Brockville, Ontario), instead of the four weak scattered companies of 1939. It was part of the Mobile Striking Force designed for the defence of Canadian territory and particularly the North, looking towards the Soviet Union. In keeping with this role, in 1949 all the units of the MSF began training

as parachute troops. Arctic exercises trained sub-units and individuals in the business of surviving and fighting in the northern wastes.

On 25 June 1950 the forces of the communist state of North Korea launched without warning an invasion of neighbouring South Korea. The United Nations at once condemned this aggression, and on 27 June the Security Council called on members of the UN to assist South Korea in resisting it. The Canadian government (and doubtless the Canadian public too) were by no means anxious to become involved in military operations in Asia, but the call of the United Nations, which it was Canadian policy to support, and the example of the United States, which at once committed forces to the conflict, could scarcely be disregarded. Canadian naval vessels were sent to Korean waters, and on 7 August it was announced that Canada would raise a Canadian Army Special Force, a brigade group in strength, that could be used to fulfil Canada's international obligations either in Europe (under the North Atlantic Treaty) or in Asia. It was assumed that many veterans of the war that had ended only five years before would volunteer, and this proved to be the case.

The new formation was to be established within the framework of the Active (Regular) Force, and its three infantry battalions were to be units of the three old regular regiments. Thus The Royal Canadian Regiment acquired a new 2nd Battalion, to which the old (now 1st) Battalion contributed key personnel, just as had happened in 1899. But the 2nd's departure for Korea was delayed. The government had hoped that one battalion would be enough for that theatre and the Patricias got the call, landing at Pusan in December 1950. The balance of the new brigade went to Fort Lewis, Washington, for training. But the intervention of China on the side of North Korea made the situation in the Far East much more serious, and inevitably the United Nations command (headed by the American general Douglas MacArthur) wanted the whole Canadian force. In February 1951 it was announced that the entire 25th Brigade Group (as it was now called) would go to Korea; and shortly afterwards another brigade was formed for service under NATO in Europe. The 2nd Battalion, Royal Canadian Regiment, commanded by Lt.-Col. R.A. Keane, reached Pusan on 5 May.

By the time the brigade entered the line later that month, the tide of battle, which in the earlier stages had ebbed and flowed up and down the Korean peninsula, had largely lost its force, and throughout the period of The Regiment's operations there the front, running across the country not far from the 38th parallel, which separated North from South Korea, remained basically stable. On this "strange battleground" of rice paddies and razorback ridges, the opposing forces fought a war of minor but often fierce operations, raids, and patrols, while UN and North Korean negotiators engaged in apparently endless discussions over a cease-fire. Late in July 1951 the Canadian brigade group became part of the Commonwealth Division, in which units from all over the Commonwealth (the United Kingdom making the largest contribution) served agreeably together. In the words of the Canadian official historian, "Under the firm, cheerful and imaginative guidance of successive British commanders, the division achieved a remarkable degree of homogeneity."

The 2nd Battalion's first serious engagement was at Chail-li on 30 May 1951. It took the village, but was so isolated from support that it was ordered to withdraw, having suffered 31 casualties. In Operations "Minden" and "Commando" in September and October, the brigade pushed forward several miles to improve the U.N. positions. By the spring of 1952 a policy had been developed by which Canadian units in Korea were relieved ("rotated") after a year of service there, and in April the 2nd Battalion was replaced by the 1st, under Lt.-Col. P.R. Bingham. At the same time Brigadier M.P. Bogert, an officer of The Regiment, took command of the 25th Brigade Group. That spring there was active patrolling, which produced little result but casualties. In June, The Regiment provided a company for guard duty at a prisoner of war camp on Koje Island, where there had been serious disorders. The Canadians had no trouble there, though the affair caused some concern in Ottawa. On 23 October the Chinese made a fierce night attack on B Company's position; some ground was lost, and though it was recovered by a counterattack the affair cost 75 casualties.

The expansion of the army had produced a 3rd Battalion of The Regiment, commanded by Lt.-Col. K.L. Campbell. This battalion relieved the 1st in Korea in the spring of 1953. The war was now finally running down, but the 3rd Battalion had one violent engagement on 2–3 May, when the Chinese attacked C Company in its positions near Chinchon. The attack was beaten back, but the battalion had 60 casualties, 25 of them fatal. In July an armistice agreement was signed and the long-awaited cease-fire came into effect on 27 July. The Royal Canadian Regiment had taken 560 casualties in this curious little war in a corner of the world remote from Canada; 117 of its officers and men had lost their lives. The 3rd Battalion left Korea in March 1954 and the last Canadian soldiers returned home in June 1957.

Before The Regiment's time in Asia ended, a new period of duty in Europe began. Canadians had been there again since 1951, when the brigade group raised for the purpose, largely through the agency of Reserve Force units, went to West Germany to serve under NATO. When these units were relieved in 1953, the 2nd Battalion, Royal Canadian Regiment was part of the relieving force. It took up quarters in Fort York, a new Canadian camp near Soest, and began intensive training with the rest of the Canadian brigade under the British Army of the Rhine.

In January 1953, The Regiment, represented by the 2nd Battalion, returned to London, Ontario, its pre-1939 headquarters and one of its earliest stations. London marked the occasion by presenting The Regiment with the freedom of the city. Later that year London was designated as The Regiment's home station and the location of the regimental depot. In 1954 another strong link with the city was forged. Its old militia infantry regiment, The Canadian Fusiliers (City of London Regiment), was amalgamated with the Oxford Rifles to form The London and Oxford Fusiliers, which became the 3rd Battalion, The Royal Canadian Regiment. Of the two militia regiments amalgamated at this time, the Oxford Rifles had been organized in 1863

and the Canadian Fusiliers in 1866; between them they perpetuated the 1st, 33rd, 71st, 142nd and 168th Battalions of the Canadian Expeditionary Force of 1914–18. Both were mobilized in 1942, and the Fusiliers in the next year took part in the expedition against Kiska in the Aleutian Islands as a unit of the 13th Canadian Infantry Brigade Group. Since 1954 The Royal Canadian Regiment has been a militia as well as a regular regiment. The London and Oxford Fusiliers are now its 4th Battalion. The new connection brought The Regiment a second alliance with the British Army — with The Royal Fusiliers (City of London Regiment), who, in the reorganized army, are part of The Royal Regiment of Fusiliers.

Finally, in 1953 The Regiment welcomed a new Colonel in Chief. The Duke of Connaught had died in 1941, and had had no successor for twelve years. Now Field Marshal HRH the Prince Philip, Duke of Edinburgh, K.G., the consort of the new sovereign, Her Majesty Queen Elizabeth II, honoured The Regiment by accepting the appointment. He has continued to honour it since that time by his constant interest in its welfare.

A platoon prepares to advance, Korea.

Major Donald Holmes leads his men on patrol.

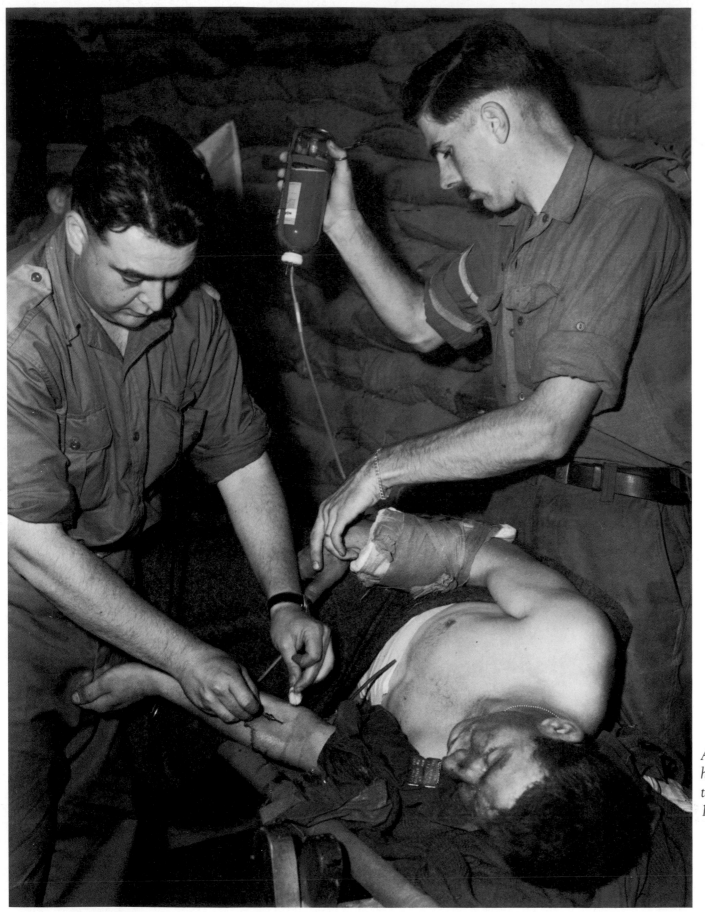

A unit medical officer and his assistant ministering to a battle casualty, Korea, 1951.

*The morning after
a night patrol.*

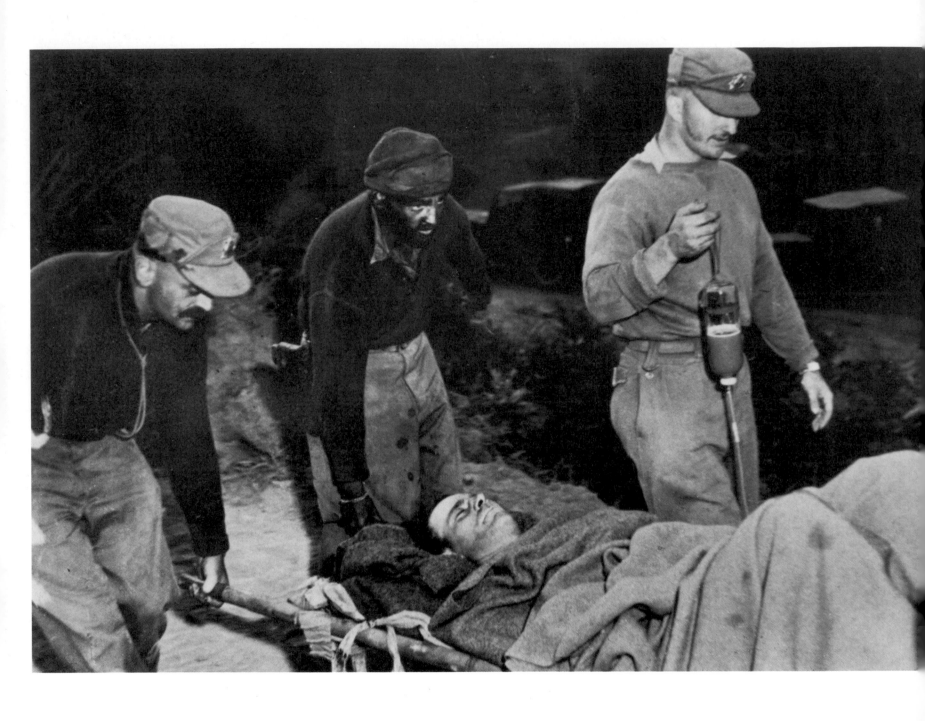

"That spring there was active patrolling, which produced little result but casualties."

A wounded prisoner, Korea, 1951.

First aid is given to a captured Chinese soldier.

June 1951. ". . . The Regiment provided a company for guard duty at a prisoner of war camp on Koje Island, where there had been serious disorders. The Canadians had no trouble there. . ."

The Demontfort twins, Korea, 1952.

K.P. duty.

A friendly moment.

A reminder of home.

VII
IN A WORLD
OF CHANGE

It remains to say something of the part that The Regiment has played and is playing in the world of new challenges and varied menaces that confronts the present generation.

The years since the Second World War have witnessed changes that the founders of The Royal Canadian Regiment would have thought unbelievable. The British Empire that dominated their world has vanished. Canada has assumed a national status that they could hardly have foreseen. We live under the shadow of the atomic bomb, as we have since 1945. Two superpowers, the United States and the Soviet Union, confront each other across the globe; two power combinations, the North Atlantic Treaty Organization (including Canada and Britain) and the Warsaw Pact nations, eye each other warily. Technological progress has produced new weapons of staggering power on land, sea, and air.

We have seen something of the effects upon Canadian defence policy of the cold war in Europe and the Korean War in Asia. A major result was the expansion of the army, which from three regular battalions of infantry in 1950 grew to fifteen in 1954. A new four battalion Regiment of Canadian Guards came into existence; the 3rd Battalion of The Royal Canadian Regiment became the 1st Battalion of the Guards. Two old militia regiments, The Queen's Own Rifles of Can-

ada and The Black Watch (Royal Highland Regiment) of Canada, each acquired two regular battalions. But those familiar with Canadian history were not surprised when government policy changed again and the military forces became the target of retrenchment. The Canadian Guards passed out of existence, as did the regular units of the Queen's Own and the Black Watch. In July 1970 the 1st Battalion of the Black Watch became the 2nd Battalion of The Royal Canadian Regiment. Since that time the three pre-1939 regiments have again been the only standard infantry regiments of the Canadian army; and The Regiment has had three standard regular battalions.

The most extraordinary development was the "unification" of the three fighting services in 1965, a measure that would have been inconceivable in a country possessing a more developed and sophisticated public opinion in military matters. It is a notable fact, however, that the "reformers" felt obliged to stop short of laying hands on the regimental system in the infantry and the armoured corps. In both the regular force and the militia the old regiments continue to exist, cherishing the traditions and the battle honours that have always been their inspiration and that would be a chief source of strength to the country in any future time of need.

Canada has no empire, but during the last generation her regular regiments have performed around the world a variety of tasks that recalls those of the British Army in times past. The European commitment to the North Atlantic Treaty Organization has been a constant since 1951, and the battalions of The Royal Canadian Regiment have continued to be well known in West Germany, while battalions of The Regiment based in Canada have more than once flown to Norway to practise the defence of NATO's northern flank. Peacekeeping tasks on behalf of the United Nations have been numerous in these turbulent years. In 1964 the violent feud between Turks and Greeks in Cyprus brought a Canadian force to that island. This, it was hoped, would be a short-term job, but at the moment of writing Canadian troops are still there. The Regiment first became involved in 1966, when the 1st Battalion left for a six month Cyprus tour. Such tours, entailing work that is always delicate and often dangerous, have been a regular part of The Regiment's experience since that time.

Training has been varied to an extent that would have made the pre-1939 members of The Regiment open their eyes very wide. Thus in March 1971 the 2nd Battalion carried out an exercise ("Nimrod Caper III") in Jamaica, practising long-range air movement, tropical living, and jungle fighting. In striking contrast are the winter exercises in northern Norway in which the 1st Battalion has taken part along with forces of other NATO nations — "Arctic Express" in February and March 1978, and more recently, in March 1982, when 14 000 NATO soldiers and airmen engaged in manoeuvres almost 150 miles north of the Arctic Circle, rehearsing a defence against a possible Soviet invasion. "Join the army and see the world" is plain truth in Canada today.

"Aid to the civil power," we know, is an old phrase in The Regiment's lexicon of duties. It appeared in a new form in October 1970, when there was extraor-dinary news from Montreal. Two kidnappings — one of which issued in cold-blooded murder — were carried out by small groups of organized terrorist fanatics. No such thing had happened in Canada before. Nobody knew how extensive the conspiracy might be. Quebec, and Canada at large, were shaken to the core. The national government, at the request of that of Quebec, took firm action. Whether it was really necessary to invoke the War Measures Act need not be discussed here; but it cannot be doubted that there was a very urgent need for a show of strength. And, luckily, the strength was there. Operation "Ginger" began. Air transport made possible a feat that an earlier generation would have thought wizardry. From across the country, the regiments and battalions came winging in: among them, the 1st Battalion of The Royal Canadian Regiment from London (just back from Cyprus), which went to Ottawa, and the 2nd Battalion from Gagetown, New Brunswick, which went to Montreal, the centre of the disturbance. And with the army in the streets of Montreal the unprecedented crisis ended. Confidence returned, and good citizens, French-speaking and English-speaking, breathed freely again. Not a shot was fired — but except in time of actual war the military forces have never rendered Canada such yeoman service.

A word must be said about the distinguished officers who — under the royal Colonel in Chief — have been the titular heads of The Regiment. The office of Colonel of The Regiment (an honorary distinction borrowed from the British Army, which however uses the word *Colonel* by itself), originated in 1959, when General Charles Foulkes was appointed. He was succeeded in 1965 by Maj.-Gen. D.C. Spry, who in turn was succeeded by Maj.-Gen. T.E.D'O. Snow. The present Colonel of The Regiment is Colonel T.F.G. Lawson, a son of the hero of Hong Kong.

On parade, 1953.

Canadian contingent at the coronation of Queen Elizabeth, London, England.

Troops parachuting over Camp Borden, 1953.

Exercise at Mohnesee,
West Germany, 1955.

Soldier and friend, West
Germany, 1954.

Soldiers in Europe training with battlefield simulation.

Farewell to Soest, West Germany, 1969.

Sergeant Dan Boudreau,
career soldier.

FLQ crisis, October 1970: guarding a cabinet minister's home.

*Participating in unit
battle-efficiency training.*

*After a long,
long march.*

West Germany, 1970s.

West Germany, 1970s.

Troops of The Regiment training in the Black Forest region, West Germany, 1970s.

Training with live ammunition, West Germany, 1970s.

The Colonel in Chief inspects his regiment, Ottawa, 1973.

The Queen and Prince Philip inspecting a Guard of Honour from The Royal Canadian Regiment, Ottawa, 1973.

Amphibious personnel carrier.

Co-operating with the German army, late 1970s.

New Leopard tank and American Cobra helicopter, 1979.

Watermanship training, West Germany.

84 mm night firing, Gagetown, 1975.

A UN position looking across the green line to a Turkish position, Nicosia, Cyprus.

Canadian observation post, Nicosia, Cyprus.

Members of The Regiment
in an air mobile assault
as part of NATO exercises
in Norway.

B Company attacking
U.S. tanks in games in
Norway.

Guided anti tank weapon defending a ridge line during exercises in Norway.

Preparing to move from a blocking position, Norway, March 1982.

B Company attacking U.S. tanks in games in Norway.

King Olaf of Norway greets members of The Royal Canadian Regiment, March 1982.

Reconnaissance flight, northern Norway.

Overleaf: B Company at services in Norway.

"Where it is needed, there it will be . . ."

EPILOGUE

A REGIMENT OF THE LINE

The infantry. What Oliver Cromwell used to call, sympathetically, "the poor foot." Cromwell was a cavalryman in the days when the man with the big horse and the long sword ruled the battle. The poor foot were musketeers equipped with clumsy and inefficient firearms and needing pikemen to protect them against the charging horsemen. But not long after Cromwell's time the musket was improved and some anonymous genius invented the bayonet. Every musketeer became his own pikeman and the infantry's firepower grew enormously. At that point the cavalry ceased to be queen of the battlefield. A new sovereign took the throne — with mud on her boots.

We all know that battles and wars are won by co-operation: co-operation between land, sea, and air, co-operation between the various fighting arms and the supporting services on the ground. But at least one military historian, putting together a history of the Second World War, found that the story naturally and inevitably wrote itself primarily around the infantry, the people who take the ground and hold it. The chronicle of Canada's century-old senior regular infantry regiment is warp and woof of the history not only of the army but of the nation.

The story is a record of service: service that was unassuming and often performed away from the public eye; service in four continents; service in five wars; but service also in many more obscure emergencies, never much noted and now largely forgotten. Is it fanciful to think that something of William Otter's rather austere professionalism still persists in his regiment? It has never gone in for self-advertisement; it has emphasized service rather than the gaudy rewards of service. People have sometimes noted that though many officers and men of The Regiment were decorated in the Second World War, it happened that no officer got the Distinguished Service Order. One reason was that men who might have got it did not survive; the DSO is not awarded posthumously. Another was a Regimental tendency to be backward about making recommendations for honours. One remembers an obituary that appeared in the London *Times* many years ago. It was that of an officer who was said (doubtless inaccurately) to be the only battalion commander in the British Army who had not got the DSO in the First World War. It was a distinction of which he was proud. The writer related that on one occasion a stranger officer, visiting this colonel, was surprised by the absence of letters after his name. He paused at the barrack gate and interrogated the sentry. Did Colonel Snooks have no decorations attached to his name? DSO, MC, OBE, or something? The sentry was mildly scandalized. He replied, "Oh no, sir; 'e's just a fightin' officer." So let

179

it be with The Royal Canadian Regiment. It is a fighting regiment; a regiment of the line. Many honours have come to it and to its officers and men, but it has not devoted itself to seeking them.

One other point. The Royal Canadian Regiment is a national regiment. It is not a county regiment, nor a city regiment — though it has warm links with many cities. Its constituency is Canada. A very characteristic incident in its history is that of 1899, when its battalion for South Africa was recruited, as we have said, "from Charlottetown to Victoria." It is proud that many French-speaking Canadians have served in it, as it is proud of the many other national strains who serve in it today. It has been, and is, a microcosm of the Canadian community.

These are perilous and uncertain times. In such days, a country is fortunate to have at its command resources like The Royal Canadian Regiment. As its centenary is marked, The Regiment continues to serve, in Canada and around the globe, as it has served since it was called into existence at the height of Queen Victoria's reign. Where it is needed, there it will be; living up to its old simple motto, *Pro Patria.*

BOOKS ABOUT THE REGIMENT

The Regimental history is in two volumes: R.C. Fetherstonhaugh, *The Royal Canadian Regiment, 1883–1933* (1936; reprinted, Fredericton, 1981); and G.R. Stevens, *The Royal Canadian Regiment, Volume Two, 1933–1966* (London, Ontario, 1967). Part of the history of the 4th Battalion, The London and Oxford Fusiliers, is told in Francis B. Ware, *The Story of the Seventh Regiment, Fusiliers, of London, Canada, 1899 to 1914* (London, 1945). The official histories of The Regiment's campaigns are G.W.L. Nicholson, *Canadian Expeditionary Force, 1914–1919* (Ottawa, 1964); the same author's *The Canadians in Italy, 1943–1945* (Ottawa, 1956); C.P. Stacey, *Six Years of War* (Ottawa, 1955) and *The Victory Campaign* (Ottawa, 1960); and H.F. Wood, *Strange Battleground:*

The Operations in Korea and Their Effects on the Defence Policy of Canada (Ottawa, 1966). See also: Department of Militia and Defence, *Supplementary Report: Organization, Equipment, Despatch and Service of the Canadian Contingents during the War in South Africa, 1899–1900* (Ottawa, 1901); Desmond Morton, *The Canadian General: Sir William Otter* (Toronto, 1974) and *The Last War Drum: The North West Campaign of 1885* (Toronto, 1972); Strome Galloway, *"55 Axis": With the Royal Canadian Regiment, 1939–1945* (Montreal, 1946) and *The General Who Never Was* (Belleville, Ontario, 1981). The best account of the Yukon Field Force is an article by Arthur L. Disher, "The Long March of the Yukon Field Force," *The Beaver*, Autumn 1962.

CREDITS

p. 1, Public Archives Canada C31378; *p. 12*, Public Archives Canada C31372; *p. 16*, RCR Museum; *p. 19*, Public Archives Canada C31366; *p. 20*, New Brunswick Provincial Archives; *p. 21*, New Brunswick Provincial Archives; *p. 22*, Nova Scotia Archives; *p. 23 top*, Public Archives Canada C31393; *p. 23 bottom*, Public Archives Canada C31442; *p. 24*, Nova Scotia Provincial Archives 13654; *p. 25*, College Militaire Royal, St. Jean, P.Q.; *p. 26*, Public Archives Canada C31352; *p. 27*, RCR Museum; *p. 28 top*, Public Archives Canada C4864; *p. 28 bottom*, Public Archives Canada C4594; *p. 29*, Public Archives Canada C3450; *p. 30 top*, RCR Museum 14-3015-1840/919; *p. 30 bottom*, Nova Scotia Provincial Archives; *p. 31*, RCR Museum; *p. 32*, Buchan–Kaye Collection, Fredericton, N.B.; *p. 33*, RCR Museum 14-3015-1840/22; *p. 34*, Glenbow Archives, Calgary, NA-3755-34; *p. 38*, RCR Museum; *p. 39*, Glenbow Archives, Calgary, NA-3755-15; *p. 40*, Glenbow Archives, Calgary, NA-3755-31; *p. 41*, Glenbow Archives, Calgary, NA-3755-70; *p. 42*, Glenbow Archives, Calgary, NA-3755-43; *p. 43 top*, Glenbow Archives, Calgary, NA-3755-63; *p. 43 bottom*, Glenbow Archives, Calgary, NA-3755-59; *p. 44 top*, Glenbow Archives, Calgary, NA-3755-73; *p. 44 bottom*, Glenbow Archives, Calgary, NA-3755-45; *p. 45*, RCR Museum; *p. 46*, College Militaire Royal, St. Jean, P.Q.; *p. 50*, Public Archives Canada C7984; *p. 51*, New Brunswick Museum; *p. 52*, Buchan–Kaye Collection, Fredericton, N.B.; *p. 53*, New Brunswick Provincial Archives 00484; *p. 54*, RCR Museum; *p. 55*, New Brunswick Provincial Archives; *pp. 56-57*, Public Archives Canada C6097; *p. 58*, RCR Museum; *p. 59 top*, RCR Museum; *p. 59 bottom*, Buchan–Kaye Collection, Fredericton, N.B.; *p. 60*, Nova Scotia Provincial Archives; *p. 61*, Buchan–Kaye Collection, Fredericton, N.B.; *p. 62*, New Brunswick Museum 00304-E; *p. 66*, Buchan–Kaye Collection, Fredericton, N.B.; *p. 67*, City of Toronto Archives; *p. 68*, National Film Board of Canada, WWI, 1910-FG-14-62; *p. 69*, RCR Museum 14-847-1907; *p. 70*, National Film Board of Canada 1910-FG-14-56; *p. 71*, RCR Museum 14-847-1907; *p. 72 top*, National Film Board of Canada 1910-FG-14-23; *p. 72 bottom*, National Film Board of Canada 1910-FG-14-23; *p. 73*, Kings County Museum, Sussex, N.B.; *p. 74*, RCR Museum 14-847-1907; *p. 75*, RCR Museum; *p. 76*, RCR Museum; *p. 77*, Milton F. Gregg Collection; *p. 78*, National Film Board of Canada 1910-FG-14-23; *p. 79 top*, Milton F. Gregg Collection; *p. 79 bottom*, Kings County Museum, Sussex, N.B.; *p. 80*, Milton F. Gregg Collection; *p. 81*, College Militaire Royal, St. Jean, P.Q.; *p. 82*, Nova Scotia Army Museum; *p. 87 top*, RCR Museum; *p. 87 bottom*, City of Toronto Archives; *p. 88*, City of Toronto Archives; *p. 89*, Milton F. Gregg Collection; *p.*

90 *top*, courtesy of D.C. Spry; *p. 90 bottom*, New Brunswick Museum 00304; *p. 91*, courtesy of A.S.A. Galloway; *p. 92*, Milton F. Gregg Collection; *p. 93*, courtesy of A.S.A. Galloway; *p. 94 top*, Public Archives Canada 23160; *p. 94 bottom*, Public Archives Canada 22523; *p. 95 top*, Public Archives Canada 23626; *p. 95 bottom*, Public Archives Canada 23123-N; *p. 96*, Public Archives Canada 31783; *p. 97 top*, Public Archives Canada 25463; *p. 97 bottom*, Public Archives Canada 22035; *p. 98*, RCR (Officers' Mess) 14-347-1939; *p. 99*, RCR (Officers' Mess) 14-347-1939; *p. 100*, Public Archives Canada; *p. 101*, Public Archives Canada 25519; *p. 102 top*, Public Archives Canada 25148; *p. 102 bottom*, Public Archives Canada 23913; *p. 103*, Public Archives Canada 25671; *pp. 104-105*, Public Archives Canada C40103; *pp. 106, 111, 112, 113, 114*, National Film Board of Canada: *Road to Ortona*; *p. 115*, Public Archives Canada 28596; *p. 116*, Public Archives Canada 37629; *p. !17*, Public Archives Canada 25868; *p. 118*, Public Archives Canada 27599; *p. 119*, Public Archives Canada 23809; *p. 120*, Public Archives Canada BJG46881; *p. 121*, Public Archives Canada KB47631; *p. 122*, Public Archives Canada JHS47286; *p. 123*, Public Archives Canada AMS49720; *p. 124*, Public Archives Canada AMS49711; *p. 125*, Public Archives Canada JHS47285; *p. 126*, National Film Board of Canada 1940WWII20FG; *p. 127*, Public Archives Canada 49708; *p. 128*, Public Archives Canada KB47629; *p. 129*, Public Archives Canada 42102KB; *p. 130*, Public Archives Canada MMO49147; *p. 131 left*, Public Archives Canada 52163AMS; *p. 131 right*, Public Archives Canada 52166AMS; *p. 132*, RCR Museum 14-1349-1951 1957; *p. 136*, Public Archives Canada SF9808; *p. 137 top*, Department of National Defence SF5067; *p. 137 bottom*, Public Archives Canada SF5069; *p. 138*, Public Archives Canada SF5035; *p. 139*, RCR Museum 14-1349-1951 1957; *p. 140*, RCR Museum 14-1349-1951 1957; *p. 141*, RCR Museum 14-1349-1951 1957; *p. 142*, Public Archives Canada SF3131; *p. 143*, RCR (Officers' Mess) 14-1350-951 53; *p. 144*, RCR Museum 14-1329-982; *p. 145*, Public Archives Canada Z-62762; *pp. 146-147*, Public Archives Canada SF2995; *p. 148*, Public Archives Canada SF4608; *p. 149*, Public Archives Canada SF3763; *p. 150*, 3 RCR; *p. 153*, Public Archives Canada; *p. 154*, College Militaire Royal, St. Jean, P.Q.; *p. 155*, courtesy of Brig.-Gen. D.E. Holmes; *pp. 156-157*, RCR (Officers' Mess) 14-1349-151/957; *p. 156*, RCR (Officers' Mess) 14-1349-151/957; *p. 157*, 3 RCR; *p. 158*, courtesy of Brig.-Gen. J.A. Cowan; *p. 159*, RCR Museum; *p. 160*, RCR Museum 14-1362-1963; *p. 161 bottom*, RCR Museum; *p. 161 top*, 3 RCR; *p. 162*, 3 RCR; *p. 163*, RCR Museum; *p. 164*, 3 RCR; *p. 165*, 3 RCR; *p. 166*, courtesy of D.C. Spry; *p. 167*, RCR Museum; *p. 168 top*, 3 RCR; *p. 168 bottom*, 3 RCR; *p. 169 top*, 3 RCR; *p. 169 bottom*, 3 RCR; *p. 170*, 2 RCR.

Colour photography, Ken Bell, Toronto.

Paintings p. 10, *Dawn of Majuba Day*, R. Woodville, City of Toronto and The Royal Canadian Military Institute. Photo by Ken Bell; *p. 107*, *A Night Raid*, H.J. Mowat, Public Archives Canada 8559; *p. 108 left*, *Brigadier D.C. Spry*, C.F. Comfort, Public Archives Canada 12389; *p. 108 right*, *Private J.W. Gardner MM*, C.F. Comfort, Public Archives Canada 12286; *p. 108 bottom*, *Captain R.M. Dillon MC*, C.F. Comfort, Public Archives Canada 12277; *p. 109 top*, *German Knocked-Out Tank*, T.R. MacDonald, Public Archives Canada 12296; *p. 109 bottom*, *Rimini as Approached on 'Sun' Route*, T.R. MacDonald, Public Archives Canada 13195; *p. 110*, *The Hitler Line*, C.F. Comfort, Public Archives Canada 12296.